Machines to the Rescue
Snowplows
by Bizzy Harris

Bullfrog Books

Ideas for Parents and Teachers

Bullfrog Books let children practice reading informational text at the earliest reading levels. Repetition, familiar words, and photo labels support early readers.

Before Reading

- Discuss the cover photo. What does it tell them?

- Look at the picture glossary together. Read and discuss the words.

Read the Book

- "Walk" through the book and look at the photos. Let the child ask questions. Point out the photo labels.

- Read the book to the child, or have him or her read independently.

After Reading

- Prompt the child to think more. Ask: Did you know about snowplows before reading this book? What more would you like to learn about them?

Bullfrog Books are published by Jump!
5357 Penn Avenue South
Minneapolis, MN 55419
www.jumplibrary.com

Library of Congress Cataloging-in-Publication Data

Names: Harris, Bizzy, author.
Title: Snowplows / by Bizzy Harris.
Description: Minneapolis, MN: Jump!, Inc., [2022]
Series: Machines to the rescue | Includes index.
Audience: Ages 5–8. | Audience: Grades K–1.
Identifiers: LCCN 2020042425 (print)
LCCN 2020042426 (ebook)
ISBN 9781645279198 (hardcover)
ISBN 9781645279204 (paperback)
ISBN 9781645279211 (ebook)
Subjects: LCSH: Snowplows—Juvenile literature.
Snow removal—Juvenile literature.
Classification: LCC TD868 .H37 2022 (print)
LCC TD868 (ebook) | DDC 625.7/63—dc23
LC record available at https://lccn.loc.gov/2020042425
LC ebook record available at https://lccn.loc.gov/2020042426

Editor: Jenna Gleisner
Designer: Molly Ballanger

Photo Credits: Delmas Lehman/Shutterstock, cover; filo/iStock, 1; Evok20/Shutterstock, 3; Jason Finn/Dreamstime, 4; Huguette Roe/Dreamstime, 5; ArtBoyMB/iStock, 6–7, 23tl; FashionStock.com/Shutterstock, 8–9; Marc Bruxelle/Alamy, 10–11; dagsy10/iStock, 12, 23tr; ssuaphotos/Shutterstock, 13, 23bl; ZargonDesign/iStock, 14–15; Krasula/Shutterstock, 16–17, 22l, 23br; Nyker1/Dreamstime, 18; Patti McConville/Alamy, 19; Pi-Lens/Shutterstock, 20–21; RonTech2000/iStock, 22r; Kara Grubis/Shutterstock, 24.

Printed in the United States of America at Corporate Graphics in North Mankato, Minnesota.

Table of Contents

Pushing Snow

Snow falls.

It falls on houses.

It covers roads.
What will help?

A snowplow!

The plow has a blade.

It pushes snow.

blade

It clears the road.

Now cars can go through!

This plow is small.
It clears sidewalks.

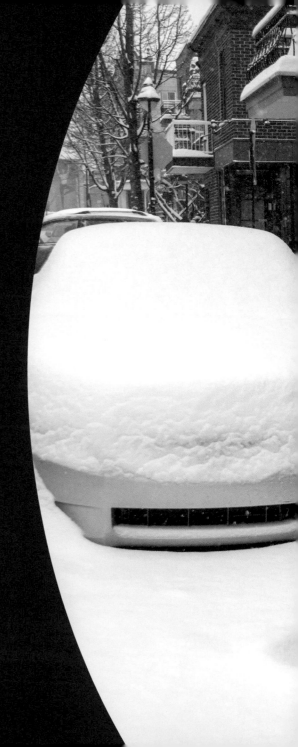

This one is big.

It clears airport runways.

Now planes can land.
Cool!

runway

light

flag

Plows have flags.

Their lights flash.

They tell cars to stay away.

This plow carries salt.

A spreader puts
it on the roads.

Why?

Salt melts ice!

salt

Plows push snow into piles.

snow
pile

The roads are clear.

Thank you!

Have you seen a snowplow?

Parts of a Snowplow

Take a look at the parts of a snowplow!

light

mirror

spreader

flag

blade

Picture Glossary

blade
The device on the front of a snowplow that pushes snow and ice.

clears
Removes things that are covering or blocking a place.

runways
Paved strips of ground where aircraft take off and land.

spreader
A machine on the back of a snowplow that drops and spreads salt or sand.

Index

To Learn More

Finding more information is as easy as 1, 2, 3.

❶ Go to www.factsurfer.com

❷ Enter "snowplows" into the search box.

❸ Choose your book to see a list of websites.